Best Buffets

Better Homes and Gardens

MEREDITH PRESS

BETTER HOMES AND GARDENS CREATIVE COOKING LIBRARY, SIXTH PRINTING

D1379023

Contents

***Out-of-the-ordinary buffet to make
you famous! See recipes, page 33.***

How to serve a buffet

Buffet-style serving is fun, whether supper is for 5 or 50! Begin with a buffet centered around good food and an attractive table. You, the hostess, will fairly glide through dinner! You can enjoy your party without shuttling back and forth to the kitchen; you'll have time to chat with the guests and they'll relax and have a good time.

Buffet serving is a natural when guests outnumber the places at your dining table. Set up card tables or small tray tables. Or let your guests eat lap-style from trays—place a stack of trays near the serving table.

Setting the table

If guests are to sit at the dining table or at card tables, have the places all set beforehand with linens, silver, glassware, and salt and pepper shakers.

For a buffet, you can go fancy and use your best china; or keep it casual with simple accessories. It's all up to you.

There's no hard and fast rule for setting a buffet. Most important: Arrange it attractively—no crowding. Place serving dishes to make it easy for guests to help themselves. Often big dishes are placed in the center at each end of the buffet table. Include a serving fork or spoon alongside each food that's offered. Place extras, such as sauce, near food they accompany.

Serving a crowd? Make twin arrangements of food, one on each side of the table. You'll avoid traffic tie-ups; self-serving will move right along.

Decide ahead of time exactly how many forks, spoons, plates, and cups you'll need and put out just that number. The food and tableware can go on the dining table, sideboard, or both.

It's time to eat!

In the drawings below, guests would begin by picking up plates and napkins. (Here napkins are stacked with plates to save room on the table; but they might be arranged beside the plates or placed with the silver.) Guests would go around the table, helping themselves to meat, vegetables, relishes, salad, rolls, and silver. If you like, either you or your husband may serve the main dish or salad to the guests.

Serving dessert

Have dessert arranged on side table; or clear buffet and arrange dessert, plates, and silver—let guests help themselves. Or pass tray of desserts to guests seated at tray or card tables. Serve coffee with either the meal or dessert, or both. Usually any beverages go on buffet or a side table.

Buffet table set away from wall

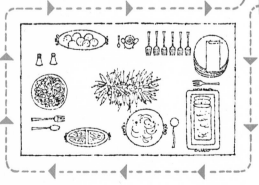

Buffet table against the wall

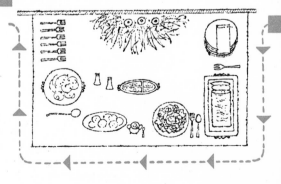

Making a party click

To help you put on a smooth-running buffet party, here are tips you'll want to keep in mind when you plan The Big Event.

Throughout this book you'll find dozens of ideas on what to serve—many recipes to fix ahead, others that keep last-minute fuss to a minimum. This frees you to greet guests, relax and enjoy your own party.

Unless you know your guests well, it's best not to serve anything that's *too* unusual. As a rule, men like simple food while women take to "something different."

When planning a dinner party, pick foods that can wait. Guests *might* be late.

You'll want to make the most of an upcoming holiday. Even just a touch—like Christmas balls sparkling among the rolls —makes the simplest meal an occasion.

Balance your guest list

Don't include everyone you know or owe at one party. The easiest formula: Invite folks who already know and like each other.

The more experienced hostess may want to try a bolder combination. Here's a tip: Aim at a balance of personalities within a framework of not-too-different interests and backgrounds. Choose some shy guests, some outgoing (and see that they meet). Your best bet: People genuinely interested in others.

Create a party atmosphere

This helps people relax and catch the mood for fun. The big thing is the setting. It needn't be fancy. Of course, the party in your living room is apt to be more formal than one in the recreation room or back yard. Make sure your table looks attractive, uncluttered. Lighting is important, too. Use lamps and the glow from candles and fireplace. Skip the harsh overhead lights.

Never put off having a party because you can't do it in the same style as someone else. Do things in keeping with your own budget and surroundings—your entertaining will have a flavor all its own.

Make your schedule flexible

It is essential to the success of a party not to plan anything that has to be done "on the dot." The good hostess keeps a finger on the pulse of her party. For instance, at a dinner party there is the "right" time to eat—the alert hostess can sense when it is, pick the moment before conversation lags or appetites become ravenous.

Plan ahead for successful party

• Organize your party early. List major jobs which must be done ahead: Decide what to serve, groceries to buy, how to set the table, when to cook the food. Plan a schedule and check off each item as you finish it.

• Serving something new? It's a good idea to try the recipe first—see if you like the flavor, if it suits the occasion.

• You'll save dishwashing if you count on smart ovenware and electric skillets that can travel from the kitchen to the table.

• Before the party, decide how to split the duties between the host and hostess.

• Budget your time—save some precious moments to relax before the guests arrive.

Buffets... all-time favorites!

High-society suppers with hamburgers and franks!

Buffet, red-carpet style, stars Chicken Royale

Easy and elegant dinner features no-carve ham!

Chafing-dish shrimp special

Hamburgers and hot dogs go sophisticated

Take your choice—all rate tops on the American poll of good eating! Duchess Franks have a surprise of ham, cheese, and pickle. Country Club Hamburgers are posh with plumed mushrooms, atop bed of peas and tiny onions. Tomato roses trim platter of "Steaks" with Caper Sauce—the filets among burgers.

High-society suppers with franks and burgers

Duchess Franks

1 pound (8 to 10) frankfurters
4 or 5 thin slices boiled ham,
  cut in half
8 to 10 thin strips sharp process
  American cheese
2 large dill pickles cut in 8 to 10
  thin strips
4 cups mashed potatoes
3 beaten egg yolks
1 tablespoon milk
½ teaspoon salt
Dash pepper

Slit franks lengthwise, not quite through.
Fold each half slice of ham lengthwise and
insert in a frank. Tuck a strip of cheese and
pickle in frank alongside.

Combine mashed potatoes, egg yolks,
milk, and seasonings. Poke two skewers
through the franks for easy handling (see
picture, page 9). Fill franks with mashed
potatoes piped through pastry tube. Place
on baking sheet; heat in hot oven (400°) 15
minutes or till potatoes are lightly browned.

Note: If skewers have wooden handles,
wrap the wood in foil; slow-broil franks
with handles extending out of broiler.

Buttered Zucchini

8 to 10 small zucchini squash, thinly
  sliced (about 6 cups)
¼ cup butter or margarine
½ teaspoon salt
Dash pepper

Put zucchini, butter, and seasonings in
skillet. Cover and cook slowly 5 minutes.
Uncover and cook till barely tender, about
8 to 10 minutes more, turning zucchini
slices often. Makes 8 servings.

Cantaloupe Sundaes

Have the melon icicle-cold. Trace a zigzag line around the melon's middle.

Now make a deep thrust with knife this
way, then that way—all around. Scoop out
the seeds. Pile center high with scoops of
vanilla ice cream. That's all!

Perfect Iced Tea

4 tablespoons tea *or* 12 tea bags
4 cups boiling water
4 cups cold water

Measure tea into teapot. Pour fresh, vigorously boiling water over the leaves. Cover
and let stand 5 minutes; stir. Then pour
brew through a tea strainer into a pitcher.
Immediately add cold water and let tea
cool at room temperature till serving time.

Pour tea into ice-filled glasses. Offer
lemon wedges and sugar. Makes 8 servings.

Note: To make cloudy tea sparkle again,
pour tea into pan and reheat (don't boil)
till clear. Remove from heat at once; add
½ cup boiling water for each quart tea.

Instant Iced Tea couldn't be easier! Fol-
low the speedy directions on the label.

Fluted Mushrooms for trim

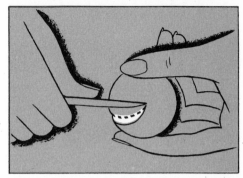

Select large, well-shaped fresh mushrooms. Wash and remove stems; drain. Hold the mushroom cap in your left hand; using a *sharp, short-bladed* paring knife, make a shallow curved cut from center of mushroom to bottom edge (see picture, page 8).

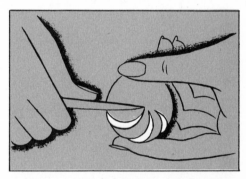

Starting at the same center point, make a second curving cut next to the first; remove strip between cuts. Repeat fluting about 8 or 9 times around mushroom cap.

Melt 2 tablespoons butter in skillet; add fluted mushrooms. Cover and cook, over low heat about 8 to 10 minutes or till tender and lightly browned; turn occasionally.

Pretty Elegant Fare!

Country Club Hamburgers
Fluted Mushrooms
Tiny Peas and Onions
Spring Salad Bowl French Dressing
Warm Sesame Rolls
Butter   Honey
Strawberry or Raspberry Shortcake
Whipped Cream
Hot Coffee

Country Club Hamburgers

2 pounds ground beef*
Blue-cheese Filling:
1 3-ounce package cream cheese,
   softened
1 tablespoon crumbled blue cheese
1 tablespoon finely chopped onion
1 teaspoon prepared horseradish
1 teaspoon prepared mustard

• • •

12 slices bacon, precooked slightly
Salt
Pepper

• • •

6 large, well-shaped mushrooms

Divide ground beef in 12 mounds. Flatten each between squares of waxed paper to ½ inch thickness.

For Blue-cheese Filling, cream the cheeses together; stir in onion, horseradish, and mustard. Top *half* the patties with filling, leaving ½-inch margin for sealing. Cover filling with remaining patties, sealing edges well. Wrap edges of each burger with bacon, using 2 slices and securing ends with toothpicks. Broil 5 inches from heat about 6 minutes; sprinkle with salt and pepper. Turn and broil about 5 minutes more or till done just the way you like them; season second side.

Flute mushroom caps—see step-by-step directions at right. To serve, top each burger with a mushroom. Makes 6 servings.

*If beef is lean, have 6 ounces suet ground with this amount. Burgers will be at their very best!

Spring Salad Bowl

1 bunch leaf lettuce, bite-size pieces
½ bunch water cress
1½ cups tiny spinach leaves
24 carrot curls
4 green onions with tops, chopped

Combine greens, carrot curls, and onions. If desired, stuff 12 pitted ripe olives with 12 toasted blanched almonds; add. Toss with French Dressing. Serves 6.

French Dressing

½ cup salad oil
2 tablespoons salad vinegar
2 tablespoons lemon juice
1 teaspoon sugar
½ teaspoon *each* salt, paprika,
   and dry mustard
Dash cayenne

Combine ingredients in jar; cover and shake well before using. Makes ¾ cup.

Rich Strawberry Shortcake

2 cups sifted all-purpose flour
2 tablespoons sugar
3 teaspoons baking powder
½ teaspoon salt
½ cup butter or margarine
1 beaten egg
⅔ cup light cream
3 to 4 cups sugared sliced strawberries
1 cup whipping cream, whipped

Sift together dry ingredients; cut in butter till mixture is like coarse crumbs. Combine egg and cream; add all at once to dry ingredients, stirring only to moisten.

Big Biscuit Style: Spread dough in greased 8x1½-inch round cake pan, slightly building up dough around edges. Bake at 450° 15 to 18 minutes or till golden. Remove from pan, cool on rack about 3 minutes. With serrated knife, split in 2 layers; lift top off carefully. Butter bottom layer. Spoon berries and whipped cream between layers and over top. Cut in 6 wedges. Serve warm.

Individual Shortcakes: Turn dough out on floured surface; knead gently ½ minute. Pat or roll to ½ inch. Cut 6 biscuits with floured 2½-inch cutter. Bake on ungreased baking sheet at 450° about 10 minutes. Split and fill shortcakes as above.

"Steaks" with Caper Sauce

2 pounds ground chuck
½ cup evaporated milk
1 slightly beaten egg
1 teaspoon salt
¼ teaspoon pepper
¼ teaspoon monosodium glutamate
   • • •
1 recipe Caper Sauce

Mix meat, evaporated milk, egg, and seasonings. Use a light touch to shape meat in 5 oval patties. Broil 5 inches from heat 12 minutes; turn and broil about 8 minutes more or till done. Remove to warm platter.

Caper Sauce: Melt 3 tablespoons butter or margarine in skillet. Drain one 2¼- or 3¼-ounce bottle capers; add capers to butter and heat. Pour sauce over meat.

Glazed Blueberry Pie

1 3-ounce package cream cheese
1 9-inch baked pastry shell
4 cups fresh blueberries
½ cup water
¾ cup sugar
2 tablespoons cornstarch
2 tablespoons lemon juice

Soften cream cheese; spread in bottom of cooled pastry shell. Fill shell with *3 cups* of the blueberries. To remaining *1 cup* blueberries, add water; bring just to boiling and simmer 2 minutes. Strain, reserving juice (about ½ cup).

Combine sugar and cornstarch; gradually add reserved juice. Cook, stirring constantly, till thick and clear. Cool slightly; add lemon juice. Pour over berries in pastry shell. Chill. Serve with whipped cream.

Plenty Swank!

Meat Balls with French Cream
Pilaf or Rice   Buttered Spinach
Spiced Orange Mold
Hard Rolls   Butter
Cream Puffs with Mint Ice Cream
Hot Coffee

Spiced Orange Mold

Drain one 11-ounce can mandarin orange sections, reserving syrup. Add water to syrup to make 1¾ cups. In saucepan combine syrup mixture, ¼ teaspoon salt, 6 inches stick cinnamon, and ½ teaspoon whole cloves. Cover and simmer 10 minutes; remove from heat and let stand covered 10 minutes to steep. Strain.

Dissolve two 3-ounce packages orange-flavored gelatin in *hot* mixture. Add 2 cups cold water and 3 tablespoons lemon juice. Chill till partially set. Stir in oranges and ½ cup broken California walnuts; chill firm in a 1-quart mold.

Meat Balls with French Cream

1 pound ground beef*
8 stuffed green olives
Seasoned flour
1 tablespoon butter or margarine
Hot buttered pilaf or rice

• • •

1 tablespoon Worcestershire sauce
2 teaspoons onion juice
½ teaspoon dried whole thyme
1 cup light cream or half-and-half
½ teaspoon lemon juice

Form meat in 8 balls, shaping each around an olive. Roll meat balls in seasoned flour. Brown in butter; then reduce heat and cook 10 to 12 minutes, turning frequently. When meat balls are done to your liking, lift from skillet and place atop hot buttered pilaf or fluffy rice.

Pour off fat; to browned bits of meat in skillet, add Worcestershire sauce, onion juice, and thyme; cook 1 minute. Add cream; cook and stir over low heat only until hot through. Remove from heat and add lemon juice. At once pour the sauce over the meat balls. Makes 4 servings.

*If beef is lean, have 3 ounces suet ground with this amount.

High-style dining—Meat Balls with French Cream atop wheat pilaf

These sophisticated meat balls are seasoned to a chef's taste! For those who wish a heightened flavor bouquet, pass a tiny bowl of snipped parsley and dried whole chervil.

Good foods and good times go hand in hand! Come to our gay red-carpet buffet—the food tastes so grand and friends clamor for the recipes!

Buffet...red-carpet style!

Fresh-cooked Shrimp

6 cups water
2 tablespoons salt
2 tablespoons vinegar
2 bay leaves
1 teaspoon mixed pickling spices
2 stalks of celery

• • •

2 pounds fresh or frozen shrimp
   in shells

Combine water, salt, vinegar, bay leaves, spices, and celery; bring to boiling.

Add shrimp (in shells, or peeled and cleaned). Cover; heat to boiling, then lower heat and simmer gently till shrimp turn pink, about 5 minutes. Drain. If cooked in shell, peel shrimp; remove vein that runs down back. For appetizer, chill; pass Cocktail Sauce. Makes 4 or 5 servings.

Cocktail Sauce

¾ cup chili sauce
2 to 4 tablespoons lemon juice
2 to 3 tablespoons horseradish
2 teaspoons Worcestershire sauce
1 teaspoon grated onion
Few drops Tabasco sauce

Combine ingredients; add salt to taste. Chill. Serve with shrimp. Makes 1 cup.

Chicken Royale

4 chicken breasts
¼ cup all-purpose flour
½ teaspoon salt
¼ teaspoon paprika
2 cups dry bread cubes
1 tablespoon chopped onion
½ teaspoon salt
¼ teaspoon poultry seasoning
Dash pepper
2 tablespoons butter, melted
¼ cup hot water
½ cup butter or margarine, melted
1 recipe Fresh Mushroom Sauce

Split chicken breasts just enough to fold. Combine flour, ½ teaspoon salt, paprika, and dash pepper in paper bag; add chicken and shake to coat.

For stuffing, combine bread cubes, onion, ½ teaspoon salt, poultry seasoning, and pepper. Add 2 tablespoons melted butter and the hot water; toss mixture gently to moisten.

Fill cavity of each piece of chicken with stuffing. Hold stuffing in by skewering opening of chicken shut with toothpicks. Dip the chicken in ½ cup melted butter; place in baking dish. (Drizzle any remaining butter over top.)

Bake in slow oven (325°) 45 minutes; turn; bake an additional 45 minutes, or till tender. Sprinkle with chopped parsley. Pass Fresh Mushroom Sauce. Serves 4.

Fresh Mushroom Sauce

Cook ½ pound fresh mushrooms (cut in half) and ¼ cup minced onion in 2 tablespoons butter or margarine till tender but not brown. Cover tightly and cook 10 minutes over low heat.

Push mushrooms to one side; stir 1 to 2 tablespoons all-purpose flour into the butter. Add ½ cup heavy cream, ½ cup dairy sour cream, ½ teaspoon salt, and ¼ teaspoon pepper. Heat slowly, stirring constantly, almost to the boiling point. Makes about 1½ cups.

Spiced Fruit Compote

Perfect hot accompaniment for chicken or ham. Or chill the fruit if you prefer—

1 No. 2½ can (3½ cups) fruits for salad
   or canned fruits of your choice
1 tablespoon vinegar
6 inches stick cinnamon
1 teaspoon whole cloves

Combine fruits (with their syrup), the vinegar, cinnamon, and cloves in saucepan; heat to boiling. Simmer 5 minutes. Garnish with a few spiced crab apples if desired. Keep hot in chafing dish. Makes 6 to 8 servings.

Buffet Salad Bowl

Nice combination of crisp, crunchy vegetables in a picture-pretty array—

½ head romaine or lettuce
2 heads Bibb lettuce or ½ head
   Boston lettuce
2 cups sliced raw cauliflower
4 medium tomatoes, sliced
1 green pepper, sliced
Special French Dressing

Line bowl with romaine. Pull Bibb lettuce apart in "petals." Arrange in bowl with cauliflower, tomatoes, and green pepper. Toss with enough Special French Dressing to coat vegetables. Makes 6 to 8 servings.

Special French Dressing

Has just the flavor zing that you like to add to a tossed salad—

⅔ cup salad vinegar
⅔ cup salad oil
⅓ cup water
2 tablespoons chopped chives or
   green onions
2 teaspoons sugar
1 teaspoon paprika
2 teaspoons Worcestershire sauce
½ teaspoon salt
½ teaspoon celery salt
¼ teaspoon dry mustard
Dash pepper

Put ingredients in jar; cover and shake well before using. Makes 1¾ cups.

Angel-cake Miniatures

These bake in tiny tube pans that can double as molds for gelatin salads or desserts—

1 cup sifted cake flour
¾ cup sugar
• • •
1½ cups (12) egg whites
1½ teaspoons cream of tartar
¼ teaspoon salt
1½ teaspoons vanilla
• • •
¾ cup sugar

Sift flour with ¾ cup sugar 4 times. Beat egg whites with cream of tartar, salt, and vanilla till stiff enough to form soft peaks but still moist and glossy. Add the remaining ¾ cup sugar, 2 tablespoons at a time, continuing to beat until meringue holds stiff peaks.

Sift about ¼ of flour mixture over whites; fold in. Fold in remaining flour by fourths. Spoon the batter into *ungreased* individual round tube pans, filling them ¾ full. (Bake any leftover batter in an *ungreased* loaf pan—use a size that the batter will fill ¾ full.)

Bake the individual cakes in moderate oven (375°) about 20 minutes. Test for doneness: Touch top lightly—if it springs back, cake is baked.

Invert cakes; cool in pans. To serve, remove cakes and fill centers with whipped cream and top with cherry, if desired. Pass Cherry Sauce to spoon over.

Cherry Sauce

Tasty-tart topping to ladle over tiny angel cakes or a cottage pudding—

1 cup sugar
1½ tablespoons cornstarch
Dash salt
• • •
1 1-pound can (2 cups) pitted tart
   red cherries with juice (water pack)

In saucepan combine sugar, cornstarch, and salt. Stir in cherries with juice. Cook, stirring constantly, till thick and clear. Reduce heat; simmer 10 minutes. If desired, add few drops red food coloring. Serve while warm. Pass sauce with Angel-cake Miniatures.

Ham—ideal for buffet!

Cranberry Punch

This luscious punch welcomes the guests, keeps any early birds happy. If you like, trim punch bowl with lush grapes—

⅔ cup sugar
6 inches stick cinnamon, broken
2 teaspoons whole allspice
1 to 2 teaspoons whole cloves
¼ teaspoon salt
1 quart bottle (4 cups) cranberry-juice cocktail
1 No. 2 can (2½ cups) unsweetened pineapple juice
• • •
1 1-pint 12-ounce bottle (about 3½ cups) ginger ale, chilled

Combine sugar, spices, salt, cranberry juice, and pineapple juice. Cover, simmer gently 10 minutes; strain. Chill.

Just before serving, pour over ice cubes in punch bowl. Carefully pour ginger ale down side of bowl. Float orange slices atop. Makes 16 half-cup servings.

Hot Cranberry Punch

To serve punch warm, omit ginger ale and add 2 cups water to juice mixture before heating; simmer 10 minutes and strain.

To serve, pour hot mixture into mugs and dot with butter. Poke in cinnamon-stick muddlers, if desired.

Jelly-glazed Ham

Carving is all done for you—

Take a shallow baking pan (or heavy aluminum foil) to the market with you. Ask your meat dealer to slice a canned ham or a boned, fully cooked ham on his slicing machine, then to tie it with heavy cord and place it in your baking pan.

Bake the ham in slow oven (325°) about 20 minutes *per pound* for small canned ham (about 6 pounds); 10 to 15 minutes *per pound* for larger ham (8 to 13 pounds).

Fifteen minutes before baking time is up, set oven control at 350° and spoon *half* the Currant Glaze over ham; continue baking about 15 minutes, basting several times with remaining Glaze. Place the ham on serving platter; remove cord.

Currant Glaze

Heat and stir ½ cup currant jelly and 2 tablespoons cooking sherry till jelly melts. Spoon over ham as above.

Fluffy Mustard Sauce

2 beaten egg yolks
1 tablespoon sugar
3 tablespoons prepared mustard
2 tablespoons vinegar
1 tablespoon water
¾ teaspoon salt
• • •
1 tablespoon butter or margarine
1 tablespoon prepared horseradish
½ cup whipping cream, whipped

To egg yolks, add sugar, mustard, vinegar, water, and salt; mix well. Cook over *hot, not boiling*, water, stirring constantly, till mixture thickens, about 4 to 5 minutes.

Remove from heat; blend in butter and horseradish. Cool thoroughly. Fold in whipped cream. (Store in refrigerator. To serve with warm meat, remove from refrigerator 30 minutes ahead.) Makes 1⅛ cups.

Sweet-potato Balls

Combine 2½ cups mashed canned or cooked sweet potatoes, ¾ teaspoon salt and dash pepper, and 2 tablespoons melted butter; stir in ¼ cup tiny marshmallows; chill.

Shape in balls, using ¼ cup mixture for each. Heat 1 tablespoon butter and ⅓ cup honey in small heavy skillet; when hot, add balls, one at a time. With 2 forks, carefully but quickly roll in glaze, coating well.

At once roll in 1 cup chopped walnuts. Place balls so they do not touch in greased shallow baking dish. Drizzle with a little melted butter. Bake at 350° for 15 to 20 minutes. Makes 10 sweet-potato balls.

Casserole of Vegetables

5 medium carrots, sliced (1½ cups)
1 medium onion, sliced
1 10-ounce package frozen
   leaf spinach
3 tablespoons butter or margarine
3 tablespoons all-purpose flour
1½ cups milk
1 cup shredded process cheese
¼ teaspoon salt and dash pepper
½ cup buttered soft bread crumbs

Cook carrots and onion covered in small amount boiling salted water until almost tender, about 8 minutes. Drain. Cook spinach following package directions. Drain.

For sauce, melt butter; blend in flour; gradually stir in milk. Cook and stir till thick; remove from heat. Add cheese, salt, and pepper, stirring till cheese melts. Place *half* the spinach in ungreased 1-quart casserole. Cover with *half* the carrots and onions; top with *half* the cheese sauce. Repeat. Top with crumbs. Bake at 350° for 15 to 20 minutes. Serves 6.

Elegant dining with ease!

Your hospitality's showing with this gala spread! A long guest list? Just double the wonderful recipes.

Peach Gelatin Ring

It's a make-ahead salad, the kind you appreciate when entertaining—

1 No. 2½ can (3½ cups) peach halves
½ teaspoon whole cloves
6 inches stick cinnamon
¼ teaspoon salt

. . .

2 3-ounce packages orange-pineapple
   gelatin
2 cups orange juice
Unpared apple or plum wedges, or
   slices of jellied cranberry sauce cut
   in 3 wedges each.

Drain peaches, reserving syrup. Add water to syrup to make 2 cups. In saucepan, combine syrup mixture, spices, and salt. Cover and simmer 10 minutes; remove from heat and add gelatin, stirring to dissolve. Let stand covered 10 minutes to steep. Strain. Add orange juice. Pour about *half* of the gelatin into a 6½-cup ring mold. Chill both portions of gelatin till partially set.

When gelatin in mold will support fruit, alternate peach halves (tipped on edge—see picture, page 19) and fruit wedges around mold, pushing fruit down into gelatin. Pour remaining gelatin over. Chill firm. Unmold on greens and circle with peach slices. Fill center with greens, if desired. Makes 8 to 10 servings.

Gingered Ice-cream Pie

Spicy ice cream gets fluffy topping of pumpkin, marshmallows, and whipped cream—

1 pint vanilla ice cream
2 to 3 tablespoons finely chopped
   candied ginger
1 9-inch baked pastry shell, cooled

. . .

1 cup canned pumpkin
1 cup sugar
½ teaspoon salt
½ teaspoon ginger
¼ teaspoon nutmeg
1½ cups tiny marshmallows

. . .

1 cup whipping cream, whipped

Stir ice cream just to soften; quickly fold in ginger; spread over bottom of pastry shell. Freeze firm. Mix pumpkin with next 5 ingredients; fold in whipped cream. Pile over ice-cream layer. Freeze.

Sea-food banquet

. . . .

Candlelight Buffet (*see cover*)

Shrimp and Mushrooms Elegante
Parsley Rice
Artichokes with Croutons
Fresh Pineapple Salad Boats
Sesame-seed Rolls   Butter
Angel Cheesecake
Iced Coffee

. . . .

Fresh Pineapple Salad Boats

2 fresh pineapples, chilled
3 oranges, chilled
1½ cups whole fresh strawberries,
   chilled
2 ripe avocados, peeled

. . .

Honey-Lime Dressing

Cut pineapples in half lengthwise—through stem portion, too. Using grapefruit or paring knife, loosen fruit from skin close to eyes to make pineapple shells. Discard core; dice pineapple.

Pare and slice oranges crosswise. Line 3 pineapple shells with orange slices, pulling slices high on sides to form scalloped edge.

Slice avocados; brush with Dressing. Toss with diced pineapple and strawberries. Heap mixture into pineapple shells. Serve with Honey-Lime Dressing. Makes 6 to 8 servings.

Honey-Lime Dressing

½ cup honey
¼ cup lime juice
Dash salt

Combine ingredients; mix well.

Shrimp and Mushrooms Elegante

The sort of rich, expertly seasoned main dish you're proud to serve to company—

   3 tablespoons butter or margarine
   2 7-ounce packages frozen shelled
      shrimp, partially thawed
   ½ pound fresh mushrooms, sliced

       •   •   •

   ¼ cup butter or margarine
   ¼ cup all-purpose flour
   ¼ teaspoon dry mustard
   Dash cayenne
   2 cups light cream
   3 tablespoons cooking sherry
   ¼ cup shredded Parmesan cheese
   Parsley Rice

Melt 3 tablespoons butter in skillet. Add shrimp and mushrooms; cook over medium heat, stirring frequently, about 5 minutes, or till mushrooms are tender and shrimp turn pink and are done. Remove from skillet and set aside.

Add ¼ cup butter to skillet; when melted, blend in flour and seasonings. Stir in cream all at once; cook, stirring constantly till mixture thickens and boils.

Add shrimp and mushrooms to sauce; reserve a few shrimp for garnish. Heat through, 2 or 3 minutes. Stir in cooking sherry and Parmesan cheese. Salt to taste.

Keep warm in chafing dish over hot water. Trim with bouquet of water cress and reserved shrimp. Serve over hot fluffy Parsley Rice. Pass extra Parmesan cheese. Makes 6 servings.

Parsley Rice

   1 cup uncooked rice
   2 cups cold water
   ½ to 1 teaspoon salt

       •   •   •

   Snipped parsley

Put rice, cold water, and salt in a 2-quart saucepan; cover with tight-fitting lid. Bring to a vigorous boil; then turn heat as low as possible. Continue cooking 14 minutes. Do not stir or lift cover.

Turn off heat; let rice steam, covered, for an additional 10 minutes. Add snipped parsley. Makes 3 cups cooked rice. Serve with Shrimp and Mushrooms Elegante.

Artichokes with Croutons

   2 9-ounce packages frozen artichoke
      hearts
   1 recipe Lemon-Butter Sauce
   1 slice white bread, diced in
      tiny cubes
   2 tablespoons butter, melted

Cook artichoke hearts according to package directions. Drain well; pour Lemon-Butter Sauce over. Meanwhile, toast bread cubes in butter; sprinkle over artichoke hearts. Makes 8 servings.

Lemon-Butter Sauce: Heat together briefly ¼ cup butter or margarine, 1½ tablespoons lemon juice, ½ teaspoon salt, and dash pepper. Use as directed above.

Angel Cheesecake

   1 cup zwieback crumbs
   2 tablespoons sugar
   2 tablespoons melted butter
   ½ cup sugar
   1 teaspoon grated lemon peel
   1 tablespoon lemon juice
   1 teaspoon vanilla
   ¼ teaspoon salt
   2 8-ounce packages cream cheese,
      softened
   5 egg yolks
   2 cups dairy sour cream
   5 egg whites
   ½ cup sugar
   1 recipe Raspberry Glaze

Crust: Mix crumbs, 2 tablespoons sugar, and the butter; press on bottom of ungreased 9-inch spring-form pan.

Filling: Beat next 5 ingredients into cream cheese. Blend in yolks, then sour cream. Beat whites to soft peaks; gradually add ½ cup sugar, beating to stiff peaks. Fold whites into cheese mixture. Gently pour into crumb-lined pan. Bake in slow oven (325°) 1¼ hours or till done. Cool about 10 minutes; run spatula around edge to loosen. Then cool thoroughly before removing sides of pan. Top with Raspberry Glaze. Chill, if desired.

Raspberry Glaze: Thaw one 10-ounce package frozen red raspberries; drain, reserving syrup. Add water to syrup to make 1 cup; blend in 4 teaspoons cornstarch and dash salt. Cook and stir till mixture thickens. Add raspberries; cool.

Call the clan for
Chicken Plate Buffet!

For this chicken dinner, there's a complete meal in each compartment—Drumsticks Parmesan, Stuffed Baked Potatoes, Bibb lettuce, radish roses. Come dessert time, place sherbets of vanilla ice-cream balls around the centerpiece of sugared strawberries in romaine basket. And, of course, pour the coffee!

Curry and go-withs,
three-decker style!

This Lazy Susan is improvised from giant brass tray and a two-story pottery serving dish! Guests spoon luscious Curry of Shrimp atop fluffy rice, then take a sample of each curry condiment. Dessert is on the second and third tiers. The mellow cheeses are at room temperature to be at their flavor best.

Streamlined suppers!

Lazy-Susan buffets

Quick casserole meals

A traditional New England feast—fast!

Do-ahead dinners— helpers are freezer and refrigerator

Lazy-Susan suppers

Why not put that Lazy Susan to work when you entertain? It can serve a whole meal, lend new drama to a guest supper—or set off a luncheon for the ladies.

Chicken Plate Buffet

Drumsticks Parmesan
Stuffed Baked Potatoes
Bibb Lettuce with French Dressing
Radish Roses   Hot Biscuits
Vanilla Ice Cream
with Sugared Strawberries
Hot Coffee

Three Decker Help-yourself

Curry of Shrimp with Rice
Curry Condiments   Hot Rolls
Assorted Cheeses and Fruits
Hot Coffee

Drumsticks Parmesan

1 cup crushed packaged herb-stuffing
⅔ cup grated Parmesan cheese
¼ cup chopped parsley
1 clove garlic, minced
8 frying-chicken drumsticks
⅓ cup melted butter or margarine

Combine herb-stuffing, Parmesan cheese, parsley, and garlic. Dip drumsticks in melted butter; roll in crumb mixture.

Place pieces, skin side up and not touching, in greased jelly-roll pan. Sprinkle with remaining butter and crumbs. Bake in a moderate oven (375°) about 1 hour or until done—*don't turn*.

Curry of Shrimp

2 tablespoons butter or margarine
1½ cups finely chopped, pared tart apples
      • • •
2 tablespoons all-purpose flour
2 to 2½ teaspoons curry powder
1 teaspoon salt
2 cups milk
2 to 3 cups cleaned cooked or canned shrimp (1½ to 2 pounds in shell)

Melt butter; add apples and cook 5 minutes. Stir in flour, curry powder, and salt. Slowly blend in milk. Cook, stirring constantly, till mixture thickens. Add shrimp, and heat through.

Serve with fluffy hot rice garnished with chopped parsley. Offer traditional curry condiments: chutney, chopped hard-cooked eggs, salted peanuts, sliced green onions, preserved kumquats, flaked coconut. Makes 5 or 6 servings.

Stuffed Baked Potatoes

Scrub 4 medium baking potatoes; for soft skins, rub with fat. Bake in moderate oven (375°) 1 to 1¼ hours. Take slice from top of each. Scoop out inside; mash. Add butter, salt, pepper, and hot milk to moisten. Beat till fluffy.

Fill shells ½ *full* with mashed potatoes. Combine 1 cup drained, seasoned cooked or canned peas and 2 tablespoons chopped green onions; divide among potato shells. Pile remaining mashed potatoes atop.

Return to oven (375°) 12 to 15 minutes or till heated through and lightly browned.

Quick casserole meals

Tenderloin-Noodle Treat

6 ounces (about 3 cups) noodles
6 slices pork tenderloin, ½ inch thick
1 tablespoon fat
½ teaspoon salt
Dash pepper
• • •
1 recipe Blue-cheese Sauce
3 tablespoons chopped green pepper
3 tablespoons chopped pimiento

Cook noodles in boiling salted water till tender; rinse; drain. Brown pork tenderloin slices slowly on both sides in hot fat (takes about 15 minutes). Season meat with salt and pepper.

Meanwhile make Blue-cheese Sauce. Combine noodles, green pepper, pimiento, and Blue-cheese Sauce. Place in ungreased 10x6x1½-inch baking dish. Arrange meat on top. Bake in moderate oven (350°) 30 minutes or till done. Makes 6 servings.

Blue-cheese Sauce: Melt 3 tablespoons butter or margarine; blend in 3 tablespoons all-purpose flour, ¾ teaspoon salt, and dash pepper. Stir in 1 cup milk. Cook and stir till thick. Add 2 ounces crumbled blue cheese (½ cup); stir till cheese melts.

Fried Corn and Onions

⅓ cup butter or margarine
2 medium onions, sliced thin
Salt
Dash pepper
• • •
2 12-ounce cans Mexican-style whole kernel corn, drained

Melt butter in skillet. Add onion; sprinkle with salt and dash pepper. Cover; cook over low heat 5 minutes, shaking skillet often. Add corn; mix. Heat uncovered 5 minutes, stir often. Season to taste. Serves 6 to 8.

Pickled Beets

¼ cup water
⅓ cup vinegar
¼ cup sugar
¼ teaspoon salt
½ teaspoon cinnamon
¼ teaspoon cloves
• • •
2 cups sliced cooked beets

Combine water, vinegar, sugar, salt, and spices. Heat to boiling; add beets. Cover and simmer 5 minutes; chill.

Oven Fruit Compote

3 firm-ripe pears, quartered and cored
2 oranges, peeled and chunked
3 medium baking apples, quartered and cored
¼ cup raisins
• • •
¾ cup brown sugar
½ cup water

Place pears, oranges, apples, and raisins in a 2-quart casserole. Combine brown sugar and water; pour over fruits.

Cover and bake in a moderate oven (350°) for 1 hour. Serve warm or refrigerate and serve chilled. Makes 6 servings.

Hearty and Homespun

Hamburger Pie
Coleslaw Combo
Pickles   Relishes
Oven-warmed Rolls
Marmalade Upside-down Cake
Coffee

Easy—your oven takes over! Cake and casserole bake at same time; rolls heat last few minutes. To cut last-minute fuss, fix casserole ahead and chill. (Allow extra baking time.)

Chef's tip: When recipe calls for a greased casserole, use a piece of bread to spread butter, margarine, or oil.

Hamburger Pie

Hard to believe that anything so simple could taste so good! It's meat, sauce, and green vegetables, all in one casserole. Take your choice of biscuit or potato topper—

1 medium onion, chopped
1 pound ground beef
¾ teaspoon salt
Dash pepper
1 1-pound can (2 cups) cut green beans, drained, *or* ½ pound green beans, cooked and drained
1 can condensed tomato soup

. . .

Potato Fluff Topper

Cook onion in small amount of hot fat till tender but not brown. Add meat and seasonings; brown lightly. Add drained beans and soup; pour into greased 1½-quart casserole. Drop Potato Fluff Topper in mounds over meat, or put through a pastry tube. If desired, sprinkle potatoes with ½ cup shredded process American cheese. Bake in moderate oven (350°) 25 to 30 minutes. Makes 6 servings.

To match picture, arrange 6 plump tomato slices alongside potato mounds before baking; sprinkle with salt, pepper, and buttered bread crumbs.

Potato Fluff Topper

5 medium potatoes, cooked
½ cup warm milk
1 beaten egg

Mash potatoes while hot; add milk and egg. Season to taste with salt and pepper.

Onion Biscuits

Another time, omit Potato Fluff Topper; top Hamburger Pie with these flavorful biscuits—

¾ cup finely chopped onion
2 tablespoons fat
1½ cups sifted all-purpose flour
1½ teaspoons baking powder
½ teaspoon salt
1 teaspoon celery seed
¼ cup shortening
1 slightly beaten egg
⅓ cup milk

Cook onion in hot fat till tender, but not brown. Sift together flour, baking powder, and salt; stir in celery seed. Cut in shortening until mixture resembles coarse crumbs. Stir in cooked onion.

Combine egg and milk; add all at once and stir just till dough follows fork around bowl. Turn out on lightly floured surface and knead gently ½ minute. Roll ½ inch thick and cut with doughnut cutter. Place circle of "doughnuts" on *boiling hot* meat-vegetable mixture; center with a few doughnut "holes"; bake in very hot oven (450°) 10 to 15 minutes or till biscuits are done. (Bake remaining biscuits on an ungreased baking sheet.)

Radish Accordions

Choose long radishes. *Without going quite through,* cut each crosswise in 10 to 12 thin slices. Chill in ice water so slices fan out accordion-style. Place in plastic bag and refrigerate till ready to use.

Carrot Curls

Cut thin lengthwise strips with vegetable-parer—rest carrot on board; pare *away* from you. Roll up long slices; toothpick to hold. Chill in ice water to crisp. Remove picks at serving time.

Vegetable Slaw Combo

8 cups finely shredded crisp
   cabbage
1 cup sliced raw cauliflower
¼ cup chopped onion
¼ cup sliced radishes
¼ cup chopped green pepper

Combine chilled vegetables. Toss with dressing. Trim salad with green pepper rings. Makes 6 to 8 servings.

Zippy Garlic Dressing

1 cup dairy sour cream
½ envelope cheese-garlic
   salad-dressing mix
¼ cup milk
1 tablespoon salad oil
1 tablespoon lemon juice
½ teaspoon salt

Combine ingredients; stir well.

Marmalade Upside-down Cake

¼ cup butter or margarine
½ cup brown sugar
Walnut halves
Pitted dates, halved
¼ cup chopped walnuts
½ cup sliced pitted dates
½ cup orange juice

• • •

1 package loaf-size yellow-cake
   mix
2 teaspoons grated orange peel

Melt butter in a 9x1½-inch round pan. Blend in sugar, spreading mixture evenly over bottom. Arrange walnut and date halves in center; sprinkle chopped nuts and sliced dates around edge. Pour juice over all.

Prepare cake mix according to package directions; stir in orange peel. Spoon over date-nut mixture. Bake at 350° for 40 minutes or till done. Cool slightly; invert on serving plate. Serve warm with whipped cream.

Hamburger Pie—fast, good

This tasty one-dish meal is dressed up for company with golden fluffs of potato and bright tomato slices.

Simple but special—

A traditional New England supper

Saturday Night Bean Feast, Posthaste!

Maine Pork and Beans
Hot Brown Bread   Chilled Corn Relish
Piccalilli   Spicy Crab Apples
Calico Slaw
Indian Pudding   Cream
or Oven-warm Mince Pie *or* Apple Snow Cake
Hot Coffee

Those wonderful foods of the Colonists and today's New Englanders are at your finger tips—on canned and packaged-food shelves or in frozen-food cases.

So how about inviting folks over for a real New England supper? Fun for the guests and easy for you! Your meal can be as simple as this supper. The beans bake all day in a brick oven—they come to you in cans or glass bean pots. Serve with hot brown bread—from a can; with corn relish, piccalilli, spiced crab apples—all from jars.

Round out the meal with Calico Slaw and a country-kitchen dessert. Up by the caster set and spoon holder is Indian pudding with a pitcher of cream. Cooks of yester-year baked this corn-meal-and-molasses dessert for hours; yours comes glassed, is heated in minutes. Or have mince pie (from a frozen package) or mix-made cake with Apple Snow Frosting.

Old-fashioned favorites with no fuss!

Polish up the family heirlooms and get set for an easy New England supper! As old-timers would say at church suppers: A spread like this makes you wish you had hollow legs!

Calico Salad

1½ cups finely shredded crisp red
cabbage
1½ cups finely shredded crisp green
cabbage
¼ cup minced onion
⅓ cup mayonnaise or salad dressing
1 tablespoon vinegar
2 teaspoons sugar
½ teaspoon salt
½ teaspoon celery seed

Combine chilled vegetables. Combine remaining ingredients, stirring to dissolve sugar. Pour dressing over vegetables; toss lightly. Makes 4 to 6 servings.

Apple Snow Frosting

1 egg white
Dash salt
1 cup sugar
3 tart medium apples
1 teaspoon lemon juice
½ teaspoon vanilla

Use your electric mixer—this frosting takes about 15 minutes to whip to a "snow." In small mixer bowl, beat egg white with salt till soft peaks form. Gradually beat in ⅓ *cup sugar,* beating to stiff peaks.

Pare apples. Quickly grate down to core —you'll need 1 cup apple pulp; stir in lemon juice and remaining sugar. Gradually beat apple into meringue, beating till fluffy after each addition. Continue to beat until stiff and shiny like frosting. (If mixture reaches top of beaters, change to large mixer bowl so you can continue to beat in air —mixture should look like frosting.) Add vanilla. Spread on cake and serve at once. (Or frosted cake can wait in refrigerator about 1 hour.) Makes 6 cups.

To match picture (page 28): Bake 2 round layers from yellow-cake mix. When cool, fill layers with strawberry jam, jellied cranberry sauce, or currant jelly. Frost top and sides of cake with Apple Snow Frosting— takes about 4 cups. Trim with circle of apple slices brushed with lemon juice.

(Refrigerate remaining Apple Snow for a pudding dessert next day. Before serving, beat in small mixer bowl till fluffy and shiny again. Spoon into 3 or 4 sherbets and serve with chilled custard sauce.)

Take-it-easy Refrigerator

Freeze-Ahead Banquet

Shrimp New Orleans
Green Beans   Watermelon Pickles
Avocado Fruit Squares
Hot Rolls   Jelly
Banana Cream Cake
Coffee

Shrimp New Orleans

½ cup chopped green pepper
½ cup chopped onion
2 tablespoons butter or margarine
1 can condensed tomato soup
¾ cup light cream
½ cup cooking sherry
1 tablespoon lemon juice
¼ teaspoon salt
¼ teaspoon nutmeg
3 cups cleaned cooked shrimp
2 cups cooked rice
¼ cup toasted slivered almonds

Cook green pepper and onion in butter till just tender. Add soup; gradually add cream and sherry; mix smooth. Blend in lemon juice, salt, and nutmeg. Toss with shrimp and rice.

Line a 10x6x1¾-inch baking dish with heavy foil, leaving long ends. Fill with cooled shrimp mixture. Fold ends of foil over mixture; seal and freeze. When frozen, remove foil package from baking dish.

To serve: Remove foil; place frozen block of shrimp mixture in original baking dish. Cover with foil; bake in moderate oven (350°) 1 hour and 45 minutes or till bubbly and hot through. Remove foil last ½ hour of baking; top with almonds last 5 minutes. Makes 6 to 8 servings.

buffets with make-aheads!
and freezer help you out

Avocado Fruit Squares

1 large ripe avocado
2 tablespoons lemon juice
1 3-ounce package cream cheese
2 tablespoons sugar
¼ cup mayonnaise or salad dressing
¼ teaspoon salt
1 cup well-drained diced canned
   peaches
¼ cup well-drained chopped
   maraschino cherries
½ cup whipping cream, whipped

Halve and seed avocado. Peel; dice into bowl. Sprinkle with *1 tablespoon* of the lemon juice. Blend cheese, remaining lemon juice, the sugar, mayonnaise, and salt. Add fruits; fold in whipped cream. Freeze firm in refrigerator tray, 6 hours or overnight.

To serve, let stand at room temperature about 15 minutes; cut in 5 or 6 squares.

Banana Cream Cake

Stir ½ cup shortening just to soften. Sift in 2 cups sifted all-purpose flour, 1⅓ cups granulated sugar, 1½ teaspoons baking powder, 1 teaspoon soda, 1 teaspoon salt, and ½ teaspoon nutmeg.

Add 1 cup mashed *ripe* banana, ¼ cup milk, and 1 teaspoon vanilla. Mix till all flour is dampened. Then beat vigorously 2 minutes. Add 2 eggs and beat 2 minutes longer. Add ½ cup finely chopped walnuts.

Bake in a greased and floured 13x9x2-inch pan in moderate oven (350°) 30 to 35 minutes or till done. Cool thoroughly. Wrap in foil; seal tightly. Freeze at once.

To serve: Uncover and thaw in slow oven (300°) for 15 minutes. Remove cake; increase oven temperature to 350°.

For frosting, mix 1 cup dairy sour cream and ½ cup brown sugar; spread over cake. Sprinkle with ¼ cup broken walnuts. Bake 5 minutes or till frosting is set. Serve.

Feast From The Freezer!

Chicken a la King   Patty Shells
Buttered Asparagus
Sliced Peaches and Pineapple,
Berries or Grapes
Frozen Blue-cheese Dressing
Strawberry Cream Pie   Tea

Freezer Chicken a la King

A natural for a buffet! Freeze it ahead; day of party, just heat and serve—

½ cup butter or chicken fat
6 tablespoons all-purpose flour
2 teaspoons salt
2 cups chicken broth
2 cups milk
   • • •
4 cups diced cooked chicken
1 6-ounce can broiled sliced
   mushrooms, drained
½ cup chopped pimiento
Frozen patty shells

Melt butter; blend in flour and salt. Stir in broth and milk. Cook, stirring constantly, till sauce is thick. Add chicken, mushrooms, and pimiento. Cool quickly by placing pan in bowl or sink of ice water. When cooled to room temperature, pour into freezer container. Label, adjust cover, and freeze at once.

To serve: Put frozen block in top of double boiler, cover and heat through, stirring occasionally. *Or,* cover and heat over low heat, stirring occasionally till mixture is hot through.

Bake frozen patty shells according to package directions. Fill with hot Chicken a la King. Makes 8 to 10 servings.

Frozen Blue-cheese Dressing

1 3-ounce package cream cheese,
   softened
⅓ cup mayonnaise or salad dressing
1 tablespoon lemon juice
4 ounces blue cheese, crumbled
⅔ cup chopped celery
¼ teaspoon salt
½ cup whipping cream, whipped

Combine first 3 ingredients; beat till light. Stir in blue cheese, celery, and salt. Fold in whipped cream. Freeze firm in 1-quart refrigerator tray. To serve, let stand at room temperature 5 to 10 minutes. Cut in 1-inch cubes. Offer with canned peaches, pineapple, fresh berries, or grapes.

Buttered Asparagus

Cut fresh asparagus on the diagonal, making thin slanting slices, about 1½ inches long. Heat large skillet; add small amount of salad oil (few tablespoons) and when hot, add asparagus; sprinkle with salt, pepper, and monosodium glutamate.

Cook covered over high heat till just tender, about 5 minutes, shaking skillet frequently. Don't overcook!

Strawberry Cream Pie

A sundae in a coconut crust! Refreshing and simple, and you fix it ahead—

1 3½-ounce can (1¼ cups) flaked
   coconut

· · ·

1 quart vanilla ice cream
1½ cups sugared sliced fresh strawberries *or* 1 10-ounce package frozen
   strawberries, partially thawed
6 Frozen Cream Toppers

Toast coconut in moderate oven (350°) about 10 minutes, stirring often to brown evenly. Cool. Lightly press into bottom and sides of generously buttered 9-inch pie plate. Stir ice cream only to soften *slightly;* spoon into shell and smooth top. Freeze firm. To serve, spoon strawberries over ice cream and top with Frozen Cream Toppers. Makes 6 servings.

Frozen Cream Toppers

Whip ½ cup whipping cream. Stir in 2 tablespoons sifted confectioners' sugar. Place heaping spoonfuls on chilled cooky sheet. Freeze firm. Makes 6 toppers.

Strawberry Cream Pie

Even though folks "can't eat another bite," this pie will disappear in a hurry! And you tuck it away in the freezer days before the party—you needn't give dessert a thought!

Do-ahead Dinner

(*See page 4*)

Oven Chicken with Curried Rice
Chutney
Overnight Vegetable Salad
Broccoli with Lemon Butter
Butterhorns   Butter
Tangerine Chiffon Pie
Hot Coffee

Oven Chicken with Curried Rice

You can fix the rice the day before. Curry seasoning is subtle—you may want to use 1½ tablespoons curry powder—

1 cup chopped onion
2 tablespoons butter or margarine
1 cup light raisins
8 cups cooked long-grain rice (about 2½ cups uncooked)
1 3½-ounce can flaked coconut
1 tablespoon curry powder
½ teaspoon salt
2 cups chicken broth
½ cup melted butter
1 tablespoon salt
2 teaspoons paprika
½ teaspoon pepper
2 2½- to 3-pound ready-to-cook broiler-fryer chickens, cut up
¾ cup chopped salted peanuts

Day before: Cook onion in 2 tablespoons butter till tender but not brown. Add next 5 ingredients; toss to mix. Place in 17¼x11½x2¼-inch baking pan. Drizzle chicken broth over evenly, mixing lightly with fork. Cover with foil; refrigerate overnight.

Day of party: Combine ½ cup melted butter with 1 tablespoon salt, paprika, and pepper. Rub well into chicken pieces. Place skin side up in 15½x10½x1-inch pan.

Bake rice (covered) and chicken (uncovered) in hot oven (400°) 1 hour and 15 minutes or till chicken is tender. Remove foil from rice; add peanuts; fluff and mix with fork. Transfer rice to serving platter, if desired. Top with chicken pieces. Spoon some of pan drippings over. Pass chutney. Makes 8 servings.

Overnight Vegetable Salad

3 medium cucumbers, thinly sliced (3 cups)
3 medium carrots, thinly sliced (1½ cups)
1 cup thin radish slices
1½ cups thin turnip slices
2 teaspoons salt
⅔ cup white vinegar
½ cup sugar

Slice vegetables with sharp knife or salad maker. (For Oriental-style salad, make slices paper thin.) Place vegetables in groups in 13x9x2-inch baking dish; sprinkle with salt. Cover and chill several hours. Drain in sieve to remove as much moisture as possible.

Combine sugar and vinegar; stir to dissolve sugar. Place vegetables back in dish, pour vinegar mixture over. Chill several hours or overnight.

To serve, drain well. Arrange vegetables on serving platter. Makes 8 servings.

Tangerine Chiffon Pie

1 envelope (1 tablespoon) unflavored gelatin
¼ cup sugar
Dash salt
½ cup cold water
4 slightly beaten egg yolks
1 6-ounce can frozen tangerine concentrate, thawed
4 egg whites
⅓ cup sugar
1 cup whipping cream, whipped
1 9-inch baked pastry shell

In top of double boiler, thoroughly combine unflavored gelatin, ¼ cup sugar, and the salt. Blend in water. Add beaten egg yolks. Cook, stirring constantly, over simmering water till gelatin dissolves and mixture thickens slightly (about 5 minutes). Remove from heat.

Stir in undiluted tangerine concentrate; chill till mixture mounds when spooned.

Beat egg whites till soft peaks form; gradually add ⅓ cup sugar, beating till stiff peaks form. Fold in gelatin mixture; then fold in *half* of the whipped cream. Pile into cooled pastry shell; chill firm. Top pie with remaining whipped cream. Trim with fresh orange sections, if desired.

Seasonal and special-occasion buffets

Thanksgiving family feast

Just the ticket for Christmas!

An elegant salute to spring!

Easy cooking for summertime

Plan-ahead potlucks

Specials for a stag party

Thanksgiving dinner with all the trimmings!

Your turn to be hostess this Thanksgiving? Stop here for recipes you'll love! Turkey in the Straw has a crisp jacket of packaged-stuffing crumbs. Pass Giblet Gravy to ladle over. Indian Succotash couldn't be simpler! Cranberry salad makes a refreshing accompaniment. Dessert is Favorite Pumpkin Pie—delicious!

For your Thanksgiving ...tradition plus ease

To go hand in hand with family home-comings and the blessings of the harvest, here are ideas and recipes for The Big Dinner— everything from turkey to pumpkin pie! You'll find tricks galore to make it easy on the hostess; enjoyable for guests.

....

Harvest Home Buffet

Turkey in the Straw
Giblet Gravy
Wild Rice and Mushrooms
Indian Succotash
Cranberry Relish Mold
Mayonnaise Creme
Spiced Peaches   Assorted Pickles
Hot Rolls   Butter Balls
Favorite Pumpkin Pie
Toasted Walnuts
Hot Coffee

You'll be a carefree hostess! There's no last-minute carving with Turkey in the Straw! Tart cranberry salad is all made ahead of time. Piecrust could be from a mix.

....

Turkey in the Straw

1 cup soft butter or margarine
1 envelope herb salad-dressing mix
1 fryer-roaster turkey, 4 to 6 pounds, ready-to-cook weight, cut in serving pieces
1½ cups crushed packaged herb-seasoned stuffing

Thoroughly combine butter and salad-dressing mix; with spatula, spread over turkey pieces. Roll in stuffing crumbs to coat; sprinkle with paprika. Place pieces skin side up (not touching) in greased jelly-roll pans or other shallow pans. Cover pans with foil.

Bake in moderate oven (350°) 1 hour; uncover and bake 45 minutes longer or until fork-tender. Makes 6 to 8 servings.

Giblet Gravy

Place turkey gizzard and heart in a sauce-pan; cover with cold water. Lightly salt the water and add a few celery leaves and onion slices if you like. Cover pan, and simmer (*don't boil*) about 2 hours, adding turkey liver last 30 minutes.

When giblets are fork-tender, remove from heat and let cool in broth. Remove giblets and chop. After transferring the cooked turkey pieces to a warm platter, scrape the crumbs and drippings from the pans into a bowl. When fat comes to the top, skim it all off and measure ¼ cup fat back into a saucepan; blend in ¼ cup flour. Cook over low heat till frothy, stir-ring constantly.

Remove from heat and add 2 cups giblet broth. Stir smooth, return to heat and cook till gravy thickens, stirring constantly. Add chopped cooked giblets and the crumbs. Simmer about 5 minutes. Season to taste with salt and pepper.

Wild Rice and Mushrooms

1 3-ounce can (⅔ cup) broiled
  sliced mushrooms
1 can condensed beef broth
2 medium onions, finely chopped

. . .

½ cup wild rice
1 cup long-grain rice
2 tablespoons butter or margarine
2 tablespoons snipped parsley

Drain mushrooms, reserving liquid. Combine mushroom liquid and beef broth; add water to make 2 cups. In saucepan bring broth mixture and onions to boiling. Add washed wild rice; reduce heat, cover and simmer 20 minutes. Add long-grain rice; return to boiling, then reduce heat, cover and simmer 20 minutes longer or till rice is done.

Add mushrooms and butter, heat briefly; then add parsley. Makes 6 to 8 servings.

Indian Succotash

1 12-ounce can (1½ cups) whole
  kernel corn, drained
1 1-pound can (2 cups) green Lima
  beans, drained
2 tablespoons butter or margarine
½ cup light cream
Salt and pepper to taste

Combine ingredients and heat. Serves 6.

Cranberry Relish Mold

1 9-ounce can (1 cup) crushed pineapple
1 3-ounce package cherry-flavored
  gelatin
½ cup sugar
1 cup hot water
1 tablespoon lemon juice

. . .

1 cup ground fresh cranberries
1 cup chopped celery
1 small orange (peel on, seeds
  removed), ground (½ cup)
½ cup chopped walnuts

Drain pineapple, reserving syrup. Add enough water to pineapple syrup to make ½ cup. Dissolve gelatin and sugar in the hot water. Add reserved syrup and lemon juice. Chill until partially set.

Add pineapple and remaining ingredients. Pour into a 5-cup ring mold; chill overnight. Unmold. Makes 8 to 10 servings.

Mayonnaise Creme

1 cup marshmallow creme
1 tablespoon lemon juice
1 tablespoon orange juice
¼ cup mayonnaise

With rotary or electric beater, whip marshmallow creme, lemon juice, and orange juice till blended. Stir in mayonnaise. Chill.

Spiced Peaches

Speedy pickled fruit to go with Turkey—

1 No. 2½ can (3½ cups) peach halves
1 tablespoon mixed pickling spices
  or 3 to 6 inches stick cinnamon
1 teaspoon whole cloves
1 tablespoon vinegar

Combine ingredients; heat to boiling. Simmer 5 minutes. Drain before serving. Stud peaches with additional whole cloves, if desired. Serve warm or chilled.

Favorite Pumpkin Pie

*The traditional kind like Grandma used to make.
Spice to please yourself—*

1½ cups canned or mashed cooked
  pumpkin
¾ cup sugar
½ teaspoon salt
½ to 1 teaspoon ginger
1 to 1¼ teaspoons cinnamon
¼ to ½ teaspoon nutmeg
¼ to ½ teaspoon cloves

. . .

3 slightly beaten eggs
1¼ cups milk
1 6-ounce can (⅔ cup) evaporated
  milk
1 9-inch unbaked pastry shell*

Thoroughly combine the pumpkin, sugar, salt, and the spices. Blend in eggs, milk and evaporated milk. Pour into unbaked pastry shell (have edges crimped high because amount of filling is generous).

Bake in hot oven (400°) 50 minutes, or until knife inserted halfway between center and outside edge comes out clean. Cool. Garnish with walnut halves, if desired.

Note: To avoid spilling pumpkin-pie filling and to keep crust free of spatters, fill your pie shell at the oven. Mix the filling in a pitcher-bowl for easy pouring.

*See recipe for Plain Pastry, page 53.

Seasonal buffets ...

Just the ticket for Christmas!

At no other time of year is it so easy to have a dazzling buffet. Takes just a few tricks to add a festive note—like holly sprigs atop the chicken casserole, and tree ornaments twinkling among the rolls. Pretty and dramatic!

Holiday Supper

Savory Chicken Scallop   Mushroom Sauce
Asparagus Salad with French Mayonnaise
Parade-of-the-fruits Tray   Buttered Hot Rolls
Ice-cream "Trees"   Macaroons
Candies   Walnuts   Divinity
Hot Coffee   Cream and Sugar

On with the green tablecloth, the little red trees, the Christmas napkins, the red-bordered plates—all to set a pretty stage for this luscious supper. To save steps, get out trays that hold enough for the crowd.

Say Merry Christmas with a gala buffet!

The star of your supper is Savory Chicken Scallop—perfect for a carefree hostess! The fruit tray, a jewel itself, makes a light refresher to accompany the casserole. Hot rolls and a big platter of asparagus salad bundles round out this easy-to-manage meal.

Savory Chicken Scallop

4 cups diced cooked chicken
3 cups fine soft bread crumbs
1½ cups cooked rice
¾ cup chopped onion
¾ cup chopped celery
⅓ cup chopped pimiento
¾ teaspoon salt
¾ teaspoon poultry seasoning
1½ cups chicken broth*
1½ cups milk
4 slightly beaten eggs

• • •

1 recipe Creamy Mushroom Sauce

Combine all ingredients, except Mushroom Sauce. Spoon into 9x13-inch baking dish. Bake in moderate oven (350°) 50 to 55 minutes or till knife inserted comes out clean. Cut in squares. Serve with Creamy Mushroom Sauce. Makes 12 servings.

*Or use canned chicken consomme or chicken bouillon cubes dissolved in hot water according to label directions.

Creamy Mushroom Sauce

1 can condensed cream of mushroom
   soup
¼ cup milk
1 cup dairy sour cream

In saucepan combine ingredients. Heat and stir till hot through.

Asparagus Salad with French Mayonnaise

Cooked frozen or canned asparagus
Garlic salad dressing
Crisp lettuce
Pimiento
Onion rings

• • •

French Mayonnaise

Drain asparagus. Pour a little garlic dressing over and place in refrigerator about 1 hour; turn asparagus occasionally.

To serve, drain asparagus and arrange in bundles of 3 or 4 on lettuce-lined tray. Top each bundle with strip of pimiento cut in V-shape. Center tray with row of onion rings. Pass French Mayonnaise.

French Mayonnaise: Blend equal parts of French dressing and mayonnaise.

Parade-of-the-fruits Tray

Delightful light accompaniment for a hearty main dish. Arrange on your prettiest platter—

Select several colorful fruits. On page 38, we show canned spiced crab apples, peach halves filled with Cranberry-Orange Relish, Cheese-stuffed Pears, whole apricots, pineapple slices; stewed prunes; preserved kumquats; Frosted Grapes. Add Frosty Stuffed Figs, if you like. Drain canned or stewed fruits and chill. Arrange fruits on lettuce-lined platter.

Cheese-stuffed Pears

Dry drained, chilled canned pears well on paper towels. Fill hollow with cream cheese. Put a red cherry, pitted date, or fig in the center of two halves before sealing with softened cream cheese. For ruffle, pipe cream cheese through pastry tube. Use holly leaves for pear stems.

Cranberry-Orange Relish

1 pound (4 cups) cranberries
2 oranges
1 lemon
1 cup sugar
1 cup light corn syrup
Peach halves

Put cranberries through food chopper using fine blade. Quarter oranges and lemon; remove seeds; grind. Add sugar and corn syrup; stir till sugar dissolves.

Pour into refrigerator tray. Freeze to a mush (about 1 hour). Serve in peach halves. (Use remainder as meat accompaniment another time.) Makes 4 cups.

Frosted Grapes

Dip small bunches of grapes into slightly beaten egg white and drain off excess. Dip in sugar. When dry, arrange on platter.

Frosty Stuffed Figs

Slit side of soft whole dried figs and fill center with broken California walnuts or pecans; press closed. Dip bottom of figs in sifted confectioners' sugar.

Perfect ending for lovely meal!

Stack up tiny ice-cream balls for "trees"; pass sundae sauce, if you like. Add Macaroons or Divinity—dessert's all ready!

Ice-cream "Trees"

Place tiny scoops of raspberry and lime ice cream on cooky sheet; freeze firm. At dessert time pile high in sherbets to make "trees." Trim with sprigs of holly. Pass sundae sauce, if desired.

Macaroons

    2 egg whites
    ⅛ teaspoon salt
    ⅛ teaspoon cream of tartar
    1 teaspoon vanilla
    ¾ cup sugar
        •   •   •
    1 4-ounce can (1½ cups) moist
        shredded coconut, cut
    Candy decorettes

Beat egg whites, salt, cream of tartar, and vanilla until soft peaks form. Add sugar gradually, beating till peaks are stiff. Fold in shredded coconut.

Cover cooky sheet with plain paper. Drop mixture by rounded teaspoons, about 1 inch apart. Sprinkle tops with decorettes. Bake in slow oven (300°) about 25 minutes. Cool slightly before removing from paper. Cool on rack. Makes about 2 dozen.

Divinity

    2 cups sugar
    ½ cup light corn syrup
    ½ cup hot water
    ¼ teaspoon salt
        •   •   •
    2 stiff-beaten egg whites
    1 teaspoon vanilla

In heavy 2-quart saucepan, combine sugar, corn syrup, water, and salt. Cook and stir till sugar dissolves and mixture boils. Then cook to hard-ball stage (250°) without stirring. Wipe crystals from sides of pan now and then with fork wrapped in damp cloth. Remove from heat.

Pour *hot* syrup *slowly* over stiff-beaten whites, beating constantly at high speed on electric mixer (about 5 minutes). Add vanilla. Continue beating till mixture forms soft peaks and begins to lose its gloss.

Drop by teaspoons onto waxed paper; swirl each candy to a peak. If divinity becomes too stiff for swirling, add a few drops of hot water. Makes 1½ dozen candies.

Cherry Divinity: Add vanilla to Divinity; tint with few drops red food coloring. Just before dropping onto waxed paper, add ½ cup chopped candied cherries.

A salute to spring!

Ginger Fruit Cocktail

Peel 1 fully ripe banana; slice on bias;
dip in lemon juice. Combine with one 1-
pound can (2 cups) fruit cocktail, well-
chilled and drained, 1 cup fresh strawberries, halved and chilled, and 1 cup melon
balls, chilled. Cover mixture and chill.

Just before serving, pour 1 small bottle
ginger ale, chilled, over fruit. Dash with
aromatic bitters. Makes 6 servings.

Savory Green Beans

    2 1-pound cans (4 cups) green beans
    1 teaspoon summer savory
    2 tablespoons finely chopped pimiento
    ⅛ cup butter or margarine
    ½ teaspoon salt and dash pepper

Drain beans; add remaining ingredients.
Heat slowly, stirring often. Serves 6.

An elegant way to usher in spring! Trim luscious Shrimp de Jonghe with fluffy parsley bouquet, Lemonade Angel Dessert with bright daisies. Go with: Tossed salad.

Emerald Dressing

A pretty and peppy French Dressing—make it a specialty at your house—

1 cup salad oil
⅓ cup salad vinegar
¼ cup chopped onion (1 small)
¼ cup minced parsley
2 tablespoons finely chopped
   green pepper
2 teaspoons confectioners'
   sugar
1½ teaspoons salt
2 teaspoons dry mustard
Dash to ½ teaspoon red pepper

Combine all ingredients in jar or blender. Cover and set aside 1 hour. Shake 5 minutes or blend thoroughly before serving. Makes about 1½ cups of dressing.

Serve with sea food, cottage cheese, or tossed green salads.

Shrimp de Jonghe

Shrimp bakes in a robust garlic-butter sauce with bread crumbs and chopped parsley—

1 cup butter, melted
2 cloves garlic, minced
⅓ cup chopped parsley
½ teaspoon paprika
Dash cayenne
⅔ cup cooking sherry
· · ·
2 cups soft bread crumbs
· · ·
5 to 6 cups cleaned cooked shrimp
   (4 pounds in shell)

To melted butter, add garlic, parsley, paprika, cayenne, and cooking sherry; mix. Add bread crumbs; toss. Place shrimp in 11x7x1½-inch baking dish. Spoon the butter mixture over.

Bake in slow oven (325°) 20 to 25 minutes, or till crumbs brown. Sprinkle with additional chopped parsley before serving. Makes 6 to 8 servings.

Lemonade Angel Dessert

1 envelope (1 tablespoon)
   unflavored gelatin
½ cup sugar
Dash salt
· · ·
2 beaten eggs
½ cup water
· · ·
1 6-ounce can frozen
   lemonade concentrate
1 14½-ounce can evaporated milk,
   chilled *icy cold* and whipped
Yellow food coloring
1 10-inch tube angel cake

Thoroughly mix gelatin, sugar, and salt; add eggs and water. Cook and stir till gelatin dissolves and mixture thickens slightly; remove from heat. Stir in concentrate. Chill till partially set; fold into whipped milk. Add a few drops yellow food coloring. Rub the brown crumbs off cake; tear cake into bite-size pieces.

Cover bottom of 10-inch tube pan with thin layer of gelatin mixture. Arrange ⅓ of cake on top. Pour ⅓ of remaining gelatin over. Repeat layers. Chill until firm. Unmold on serving plate. Trim with daisies. Makes 12 servings.

Easy cookin' for summer

Over-the-coals Dinner

Backyard Lamb Shanks
Parsley Rice   Outdoor Hot Relish
Grill-top Tomatoes
Toasty French Bread Slices
Warm Blueberry Pie   Iced Tea

Grill-top Tomatoes: Brush tomato halves with Italian dressing; top with salt, pepper, basil, and buttered crumbs. Place cut side up on foil or greased grill over hot coals for 10 minutes.

Backyard Lamb Shanks

Marinade has plenty of tang to complement lamb—

6 meaty lamb shanks
1 recipe Barbecue Marinade

Place lamb shanks in deep bowl; pour marinade over; let stand 4 hours. Salt meat. Grill over slow coals, brushing with marinade and turning occasionally, about 1 hour or till tender—don't overcook. Heat remaining marinade; serve as a relish.
Barbecue Marinade: Combine 1 cup tomato juice, ½ cup lemon juice, ½ cup dill-pickle juice, 1 large onion, finely chopped, 1 green pepper, finely chopped, 1 teaspoon salt, 1 teaspoon coarse-cracked pepper, 1 teaspoon cumin, and 1 teaspoon marjoram. Pour over shanks as above.

Outdoor Hot Relish

Mix together 2 medium tomatoes (finely chopped and well drained), 1 medium onion (finely chopped), 1 small green pepper (finely chopped), 3 or 4 small hot pickled Italian peppers (chopped, about 1 tablespoon), 2 tablespoons sugar, ½ teaspoon mustard seed, ½ teaspoon celery seed, and ½ teaspoon salt. Cover with ¼ cup white vinegar. Chill several hours. Makes 2 cups.

Plan-ahead potlucks

Deviled Eggs

For extra flavor and color, add chopped pimiento or olives to the yolk mixture—

6 hard-cooked eggs, halved lengthwise

• • •

¼ cup mayonnaise or salad dressing
1 teaspoon vinegar
.1 teaspoon prepared mustard
½ teaspoon salt
Dash pepper

Remove egg yolks; mash and combine with remaining ingredients. Refill egg whites, using pastry tube if desired. (For plump stuffed eggs, refill only 8 of the whites; chop extras for salad next day.) Chill. Serve cold right from refrigerator container.

Devil's Food Cake

⅔ cup shortening
1⅔ cups sifted cake flour
1¼ cups sugar
1 teaspoon soda
¾ teaspoon salt
½ cup cocoa (regular-type, dry)
1 cup buttermilk
2 eggs
1 teaspoon vanilla

Stir shortening to soften. Sift in flour, sugar, soda, and salt. Add cocoa and ⅔ *cup* buttermilk. Mix till all flour is dampened. Beat vigorously 2 minutes. Add remaining buttermilk, the eggs, and vanilla. Beat vigorously 2 minutes longer.

Bake in 2 paper-lined 8x1½-inch round cake pans at 350° for 25 to 30 minutes or till done. Frost with Fast Fudge Frosting.

Fast Fudge Frosting

Combine 4½ cups sifted confectioners' sugar (a 1-pound package), ½ cup cocoa (regular-type, dry), ¼ teaspoon salt; mix well. Add ⅓ cup boiling water, ⅓ cup soft butter; blend. Add 1 teaspoon vanilla.

Beat till of spreading consistency. (If frosting becomes too stiff, add few drops hot water.) Frosts two 8-inch layers.

Good Times Yellow Cake

⅔ cup butter or margarine
1¾ cups sugar
2 eggs
1½ teaspoons vanilla

. . .

3 cups sifted cake flour
2½ teaspoons baking powder
1 teaspoon salt
1¼ cups milk

Cream butter; add sugar, eggs, and vanilla and beat till fluffy (beat 5 minutes at high speed on mixer, scraping bowl occasionally to guide batter into beaters or beat 5 minutes by hand). Sift flour with baking powder and salt; add to creamed mixture alternately with milk; beat after each addition. Beat 1 minute longer.

Bake in 2 paper-lined 9x1½-inch round pans in moderate oven (350°) 30 to 35 minutes or till done. Cool 10 minutes; remove from pans. Frost thoroughly cooled cake with Coconut Frosting.

Coconut Frosting

Combine 1 cup sugar, dash salt, ¼ teaspoon cream of tartar, and ⅓ cup water. Bring to boiling; cook and stir till sugar dissolves. Place 2 egg whites in small bowl of electric mixer. Pour boiling syrup in a thin stream over unbeaten egg whites, beating at high speed till frosting is of spreading consistency.

Add 1 teaspoon vanilla. Spread on cooled cake and sprinkle with 1¼ cups (one 3½-ounce can) flaked coconut. Frosts top and sides of two 8- or 9-inch layers.

Fresh Peach Ice Cream

Blend 1 cup mashed ripe peaches, ¼ cup sugar, and 1 tablespoon lemon juice. Combine 1 cup chilled evaporated milk, 3 tablespoons water, and 2 to 3 drops almond extract; stir in peach mixture. Freeze in a 1-quart ice-cream freezer, using 6 parts ice to 1 part coarse salt. Remove dasher.

Cover top of freezer can with several thicknesses of wax paper; replace lid. Pack in ice and salt using 4 parts ice to 1 part salt. Allow to ripen 1 hour. Or store ice cream in refrigerator tray in freezer. Makes 6 to 8 servings.

Family Reunion Potluck

Pork Chop 'n Stuffing Bake
Scalloped Potatoes
Baked Carrots   Buttered Peas
Cranberry-Orange Ring
Warm Pan Rolls   Butter
Banana-Prune Cake
Hot Coffee

Pork Chop'n Stuffing Bake

8 ½-inch pork chops
Salt and pepper
4 cups toasted bread cubes
1½ cups chopped unpared apple
¾ cup chopped celery
¾ cup chopped onion
½ cup seedless raisins
1½ to 2 teaspoons sage
1½ teaspoons salt
¼ teaspoon pepper
½ cup beef broth
1 large apple, cut in 8 wedges

Trim excess fat from chops. Slowly brown in small amount hot fat. Season.

In 3-quart casserole, or Dutch oven, combine next 8 ingredients. Add beef broth; toss lightly to moisten. Place browned chops in ring atop dressing. Cover and bake in moderate oven (350°) 1 hour or till tender. Last 15 minutes place apple wedges between pork chops. Makes 8 servings.

Cranberry-Orange Ring

1 3-ounce package cherry-flavored gelatin
1 cup boiling water
1 10-ounce package frozen cranberry-orange relish, partially thawed
1 9-ounce can crushed pineapple
1 tablespoon lemon juice
½ cup *each* chopped celery and walnuts

Dissolve gelatin in boiling water; add relish and stir till completely thawed. Stir in pineapple (with liquid) and lemon juice. Chill till partially set. Fold in celery and nuts. Spoon into 5-cup ring mold chill; till firm. Makes 8 to 10 servings.

Banana-Prune Cake

An old-time moist cake that's a good keeper (if you can hide it from the family)—

⅔ cup shortening
2½ cups sifted cake flour
1½ cups sugar
1 teaspoon baking powder
1 teaspoon soda
1 teaspoon salt
1 cup mashed *fully ripe* bananas (2 to 3)
⅔ cup milk
2 eggs
1 cup chopped pitted cooked prunes
½ cup chopped California walnuts

Stir shortening just to soften. Sift in dry ingredients. Add bananas and *half* the milk; mix till all flour is dampened. Then beat vigorously 2 minutes. Add eggs and remaining milk; beat 2 minutes longer. Fold in prunes and nuts. Pour into paper-lined 13x9x2-inch pan.

Bake in moderate oven (350°) 40 to 45 minutes. Let stand about 10 minutes and turn out of pan. When cool, frost top and sides with Brown-sugar Frosting; trim with California walnut halves.

Note: For "portable" cake to take to covered-dish dinner, bake in greased pan; frost in pan.

Brown-sugar Frosting

A fluffy 7-minute frosting with wonderful brown-sugar flavor. You'll make it often—

1 egg white
¾ cup brown sugar
3 tablespoons cold water
1 teaspoon light corn syrup *or*
⅛ teaspoon cream of tartar
Dash salt
¼ teaspoon maple flavoring

Place all ingredients except maple flavoring in top of double boiler (not over heat). Beat 1 minute with electric or rotary beater to blend. Place over boiling water and cook, beating constantly until mixture forms stiff peaks, *about* 4 to 5 minutes (don't overcook). Remove from boiling water. Add maple flavoring and beat 1 to 2 minutes or till of spreading consistency. Frosts top and sides of 13x9x2-inch sheet cake or tops and sides of two 8-inch layers.

Potluck—everyone shares the fare!

Hub of menu is Baked Pork Chops with Apple Stuffing. Round out meal with Scalloped Potatoes, Cranberry Relish Ring, Banana-Prune Cake. Make in easy-to-tote pans.

Something for the boys

Hot Mulled Cider

Spices do wonderful things for cider!—

½ cup brown sugar
¼ teaspoon salt
2 quarts cider
1 teaspoon whole allspice
1 teaspoon whole cloves
3 inches stick cinnamon
Dash nutmeg

Combine brown sugar, salt, and cider. Tie spices in small piece of cheese cloth; add. Slowly bring to a boil; cover and simmer 20 minutes. Remove spices. Serve hot. (To use glass punch bowl, first heat the bowl with warm water. Pour out water and place a large metal spoon in bowl; pour punch slowly onto spoon.) Makes 10 servings. Serve plain or with Orange Buoys.

Orange Buoys: Omit cloves from recipe above. Stud 2 oranges generously with cloves, then cut one orange in half. Add to punch at the same time as the spices.

1-2-3 Cheese Spread

8 ounces sharp Cheddar cheese,
   shredded (2 cups)
¼ to ⅓ cup light cream
1 teaspoon prepared mustard

To shredded cheese add enough cream for
good spreading consistency. Stir in prepared mustard. For best flavor, serve at
room temperature. Makes 1⅓ cups.

Hot Garlic Bread

Hot-roll mix gives you a head start—

1 package hot-roll mix
⅔ cup warm water
2 slightly-beaten egg whites
½ teaspoon salt
Yellow corn meal

• • •

½ cup soft butter or margarine
1 or 2 cloves garlic, crushed

Soften yeast from hot-roll mix in *only*
⅔ *cup warm* water. Reserve 1 tablespoon
egg white for glaze (omit egg called for
on package); stir remaining egg white into
softened yeast. Add salt and the roll mix;
blend well. Turn out on generously floured
surface (use about ¼ cup all-purpose
flour); knead 7 minutes, working in *all* the
flour to form *very* stiff dough that is smooth
and satiny. Place in lightly greased bowl;
turn once to grease top. Cover; let rise in
warm place till double (about 1 hour).

Turn out on lightly floured surface.
Shape, tapering ends, in 1 long narrow
loaf (about 12 inches). Place on greased
baking sheet sprinkled with corn meal.
Cover; let double (30 to 45 minutes). Add
1 tablespoon water to reserved egg white;
brush over tops and sides of loaf. With
sharp knife, gently make lengthwise cut,
½- to ¾-inch deep, down center of loaf.
(Place large shallow pan on lower rack of
oven; fill with boiling water.) Bake at
375° for 15 minutes; brush with egg white,
bake 15 to 20 minutes longer or till done.

Slice cooled bread on the bias, cutting
to, *but not through*, bottom crust. Mix butter with garlic; spread on one side of
each slice. Wrap loaf in foil. Heat at 350°
for 25 to 30 minutes or till hot through.

Deviled Bones

*These hearty beef bones are brushed with a
tangy sauce and flavored with hickory—*

Sauce Diable:
1 12-ounce bottle extra-hot catsup
1 tablespoon celery seed
¼ cup vinegar
¼ cup Worcestershire sauce
¼ teaspoon dry mustard
¼ teaspoon Tabasco sauce

• • •

9 pounds uncooked beef rib-roast
   bones, full length or in 4-inch lengths
Unseasoned meat tenderizer
Vinegar

Combine ingredients for sauce. Trim fat
from ribs. Sprinkle tenderizer evenly on
all surfaces of meat, as you would salt. *Do
not use salt.* With fork, pierce deeply and
generously to work tenderizer into meat
(don't forget between bones). Let stand 1
hour at room temperature.

Brush the ribs with vinegar and place
bone side down on grill. Broil, turning
often, about 20 to 25 minutes for rare.
During last 10 minutes, brush with Sauce
Diable, and toss damp hickory on the coals.
Allow about 1½ pounds beef bones for
each hungry guy. Snip between bones.
Eat in Henry VIII style!

Barbecued Loin Backs

*Marinate meaty loin ribs in a sweet-sour
sauce, then cook slowly for fullest flavor—*

4 or 5 pounds loin-back ribs cut in
   serving pieces
½ cup prepared mustard
½ cup light molasses
½ cup soy sauce
⅓ cup vinegar
¼ cup Worcestershire sauce
2 teaspoons Tabasco sauce

Place ribs in shallow baking pan.* Combine remaining ingredients; pour over
ribs. Chill 3 hours or longer. Spoon sauce
over the ribs. Bake in moderate oven
(350°) about 1½ hours or till tender and
well-done, basting occasionally. Turn once
during baking. Garnish with lemon wedges.
Makes 4 to 6 servings.

*Foil-line baking pan for easy cleanup.

Can-can Baked Beans

3 1-pound cans (6 cups) baked beans
1 8-ounce can (1 cup) seasoned tomato
  sauce
1 cup chopped onion
¼ cup brown sugar
½ cup catsup
2 tablespoons prepared mustard
1 teaspoon salt
4 drops Tabasco sauce

• • •

6 slices Canadian-style bacon

In 2-quart casserole or bean pot, combine beans, tomato sauce, onion, brown sugar, catsup, and seasonings. Bury bacon in the beans.

Bake uncovered in slow oven (300°) 3½ to 4 hours. Toward end of cooking time, fork bacon to top. Makes 6 to 8 servings.

Cabbage Bowls

To match picture on page 50, choose a large head each of red and green cabbage. Loosen the crisp, curling outer leaves of each and spread out, petal fashion.

With a sharp knife, hollow out center of cabbage to within 1 inch of sides and bottom. Finely shred center cabbage and use in slaw recipes. Heap the Green Slaw in the red cabbage bowl, and the Red Slaw in the green cabbage bowl.

Red Slaw

Combine 3 cups finely shredded crisp red cabbage, chilled, and ¼ cup chopped green pepper. For dressing, mix together 2 to 3 tablespoons sugar, 3 tablespoons vinegar, 2 tablespoons salad oil, and 1 teaspoon salt; stir to dissolve sugar. Pour over vegetables; toss lightly. Trim with green pepper rings. Makes 6 servings.

Green Slaw

Combine 3 cups finely shredded crisp green cabbage, chilled, and ¼ cup minced onion.

For dressing, mix together ⅓ cup mayonnaise, 1 tablespoon vinegar, 2 teaspoons sugar, ½ teaspoon salt, and ½ teaspoon celery seed; stir to dissolve sugar. Pour over vegetables; toss lightly. Trim last minute with slices of red apple. Makes 6 servings.

Neiman-Marcus Apple Pie

1 10-inch unbaked pastry shell*
11 cups quartered pared
  baking apples
2 cups sugar
4 tablespoons all-purpose flour
1 teaspoon salt
⅓ cup coffee cream
¼ cup milk
⅛ teaspoon cinnamon

Fill unbaked pie shell with the quartered apples. Thoroughly combine sugar, flour, and salt; add cream and milk; beat. Cover apples with mixture. Sprinkle with cinnamon. Bake in moderate oven (375°) 1½ to 2 hours or till apples are soft. (Cover pie loosely with aluminum foil for first hour of baking, then remove foil.) Serve warm with scoops of aged Cheddar.

*Use an extra-deep 10-inch pie plate. Place sheet of aluminum foil on oven rack to catch any wayward juices.

Plain Pastry

For one 9- or 10-inch single-crust pie or an 8-inch double-crust pie—

1½ cups sifted all-purpose flour
½ teaspoon salt
½ cup shortening
4 to 5 tablespoons cold water

Sift together flour and salt. Cut in shortening with pastry-blender or blending fork till pieces are size of small peas.

Sprinkle 1 tablespoon of the water over part of flour-shortening mixture. Gently toss with fork; push to one side of bowl.

Sprinkle next tablespoon water over dry part; mix lightly; push to moistened part at side. Repeat till all is moistened. Gather up with fingers; form in a ball.

On lightly floured surface, flatten ball slightly and roll ⅛ inch thick. Roll spoke-fashion, from center to edge of dough. Use light strokes.

Transfer pastry to pie plate, fitting loosely onto bottom and sides. Trim ½ to 1 inch beyond edge; fold under and flute. *Do not prick.*

(If *baked* pie shell is needed, prick bottom and sides well with a fork. Bake at 450° till golden, 10 to 12 minutes.)

Buffets for a crowd!

Ham dinner for the gang,
a take-it-easy meal! (Dessert
and salad are done day before.)

A luau—luscious foods
with a tropical lilt,
and Mainlander appeal!

Casserole supper for 24—
planned for a carefree hostess!

When it's your turn to entertain the club

Do dinner buffet-style! Guests help themselves to baked ham, take a big spoonful of scalloped potatoes (in chafing dish) and Garden Wheel Salad. Dessert? Angel Pineapple Torte.

Cooking for the gang!

Baked Ham Buffet for 16

Pineapple Refresher   Potato Chips
Glazed Baked Ham
Scalloped Potatoes Supreme
Garden Wheel Salad
Chutney Dressing
Buttered Hot Rolls
Angel Pineapple Torte   Coffee

Pineapple Refresher

Chill one 46-ounce can unsweetened pineapple juice. Just before serving, gently stir in 3 small bottles lemon-lime carbonated beverage, chilled. Shake in aromatic bitters to taste. Serve over crushed ice. Makes 16 one-half cup servings.

Garden Wheel Salad

1 large head cauliflower, cooked whole
3 10-ounce packages frozen asparagus
  spears, cooked
2 1-pound cans green beans
2 bunches (12 to 16) small carrots,
  cooked
2 10-ounce packages frozen peas,
  cooked
2 1-pound cans sliced beets

 . . .

1 medium onion, sliced thin and
  separated in rings
2 8-ounce bottles clear French dressing
1 recipe Chutney Dressing

Drain cooked and canned vegetables. Place each in separate dish. Drizzle French dressing over and chill several hours or overnight, turning occasionally.

Line large platter with lettuce. Set cauliflower in center in large lettuce cup; arrange marinated vegetables and onion rings around, spoke fashion. Serve with Chutney Dressing. Makes 16 servings.

Chutney Dressing

Combine 1½ cups mayonnaise, ¼ cup chopped chutney, and ½ teaspoon curry powder. Mix well.

Scalloped Potatoes Supreme

2 quarts thin-sliced pared potatoes
¼ cup chopped green pepper
¼ cup minced onion
1 can condensed cream of mushroom
  soup
1 cup milk
2 teaspoons salt

In greased 11x7x1½-inch baking dish or 2-quart casserole alternate layers of potatoes, green pepper, and onion. Combine remaining ingredients and dash pepper; pour over potato mixture.

Cover; bake at 350° for 45 minutes. Uncover and bake 20 to 30 minutes longer or till potatoes are tender. Makes 8 servings. (For 16, double the recipe.)

Angel Pineapple Torte

Have 9 egg whites (1¼ cups) at room temperature. Add 1 tablespoon vanilla, 1 teaspoon cream of tartar, and ½ teaspoon salt. Beat till frothy. Gradually add 3 cups sugar, a small amount at a time, beating till very stiff peaks form and sugar is dissolved (10 to 15 minutes).

Cover cooky sheet with plain ungreased paper. Using an 8-inch round cake pan as guide, draw 3 circles on the paper. Divide meringue mixture among circles; spread to make 3 smooth flat layers. Bake in very slow oven (275°) 1½ hours. Turn off heat and let dry in oven (door closed) at least 2 hours or overnight.

Fold one 1-pound 4-ounce can (1¼ cups) *well drained* crushed pineapple and ½ cup chopped maraschino cherries, *well drained*, into 1 cup whipping cream, whipped; spread between layers of meringue. Frost torte with 2 cups whipping cream, whipped. Chill 12 to 24 hours. Serves 12 to 16.

Baked Ham

Place ham fat side up on rack in shallow pan—do not cover or add water. Insert meat thermometer. Bake in slow oven (325°)—see timetable for baking time and internal temperature for your ham.

Half an hour before time is up, remove from oven and pour fat drippings from pan. Score ham fat in diamonds—cut only ¼ inch deep. Stud with whole cloves. Spoon marmalade, preserves, or the glaze below, over ham. Continue baking about 30 minutes more, spooning glaze over 2 or 3 times. Garnish with peach slices and maraschino cherries.

Glaze: Mix 1 cup brown sugar, ½ cup honey, and ¼ cup ham fat; spread over ham. Continue baking as above.

Baked-ham Timetable (Set oven at 325°)

Kind of ham	Min. per lb. (approximate*)	Total time	Internal meat temp.
Fully Cooked ham			
Whole, 12-14 pounds	12-15	3-3¼ hrs.	130°
Round boneless whole, 12-14 lbs.	18	3½-4 hrs.	130°
Cook-before-eating ham			
Whole, 10-12 pounds	18-20	3½-4 hrs.	160°
Whole, 12-14 pounds	16-18	3¾-4½ hrs.	160°

*The smaller number of minutes per pound is for larger hams, the greater for smaller hams.

Ham carving made easy! Follow these pictures—

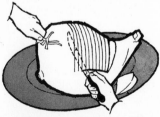

1 Bring ham to table decorated side up. Place so shank end is at carver's right. Cut 2 or 3 lengthwise slices from *thin* side—near you on a left ham, as here; away from you on a right ham. Then stand ham on the flat base you've just made.

2 Anchor with meat fork. Now remove a small wedge 6 inches from shank end; cut thin slices down to bone. *Or*, at large end, cut down to leg bone in front of bone that angles upward (find bone with skewer beforehand), and cut to leg bone at shank.

3 Run knife along leg bone. Slices already cut will be released, *or* you will have cushion of ham to lift off to platter, place cut side down, and slice.

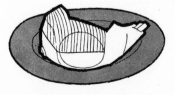

4 Time for seconds? Turn ham back to first position. Cut slices at right angles to bone as shown; slide knife along bone to release slices all at once.

Come over for a luau!

French-fried Shrimp

    3½ to 4 pounds fresh or frozen shrimp
      in shells
    2 cups sifted all-purpose flour
    1 teaspoon sugar
    1 teaspoon salt
    2 slightly beaten eggs
    2 cups ice water
    ¼ cup salad oil or melted fat

Peel shell from shrimp, leaving last section and tail intact. Butterfly shrimp by cutting almost through at center back, leaving connected at both ends. Remove black line. Place between paper towels to dry; press to open and flatten slightly.

Combine remaining ingredients for batter. Mix just enough to blend; don't overwork.

Dip shrimp into batter. Fry in deep, hot fat (375°) until golden brown, 2½ to 3 minutes. Drain. Serve with Sweet-Sour Sauce, Chinese Mustard, and Red Sauce.

Red Sauce

    6 tablespoons catsup
    6 tablespoons chili sauce
    2 to 4 tablespoons horseradish
    2 teaspoons lemon juice
    Dash Tabasco sauce

Combine all ingredients. Mix well.

Sweet-Sour Sauce

Combine 1 cup sugar, ½ cup white vinegar, ½ cup water, 1 tablespoon chopped green pepper, 1 tablespoon chopped pimiento, and ½ teaspoon salt; simmer 5 minutes.

Mix 2 teaspoons cornstarch with 1 tablespoon cold water; add to hot mixture. Cook and stir till sauce thickens. Cool, strain. Add 1 teaspoon paprika. Serve with French-fried Shrimp. Makes 1½ cups.

Chinese Mustard

Stir ½ cup boiling water into ½ cup dry English mustard. Add 1 teaspoon salt and 4 teaspoons salad oil. Serve with French-fried Shrimp.

Barbecued Pork Backs

Absolutely delicious! The pineapple-chili-sauce glaze is almost like tomato preserves—

    5 to 6 pounds meaty pork backbones
      or ribs, cut in serving pieces
    1 cup chili sauce
    1 12-ounce jar (1 cup) pineapple
      preserves
    ⅓ cup vinegar

Season meat with salt. Place in shallow roasting pan, meaty side up. Roast in very hot oven (450°) 30 minutes. Lower temperature control to 350° and continue baking 30 minutes. Spoon off excess fat.

Combine remaining ingredients; brush on meat and continue baking at 350° about 30 minutes or till done, basting occasionally with sauce. Makes 6 to 8 servings.

Note: Ribs are done when there's no pink, and meat can easily be pulled away from the bones.

Bring Hawaii to your table!

From the huge wood tray, you feast on barbecued ribs, Chinese peas, and fried rice. The upper tray offers shrimp to dip in the sauces.

Chinese Fried Rice

1 cup finely diced cooked ham,
   chicken, or pork
¼ cup salad oil
1 6-ounce can (1⅓ cups) broiled
   sliced mushrooms, drained
7 cups chilled day-old cooked rice
2 green onions, finely chopped
¼ cup soy sauce

• • •

2 well-beaten eggs

In 12-inch skillet, brown meat in hot oil.
Add mushrooms, rice, onion, and soy sauce.
Continue to fry over low heat about 15
minutes, stirring constantly.

Add well-beaten eggs and continue to
stir for another 15 minutes or until dry
enough to be fluffy. Add additional soy
sauce, if desired. Makes 16 servings.

Trader's Punch

*No namby-pamby punch this! Tingling and
refreshing as an Island breeze—*

2 cups orange juice
2 cups lemon juice
1 cup grenadine syrup
½ cup light corn syrup
3 1-pint 12-ounce bottles ginger ale,
   chilled
Fresh berries or sliced fruit

Mix fruit juices, grenadine and corn syrup;
chill. Just before serving, add ginger ale
and fruit. Makes 4 quarts.

Chinese Peas and Chicken

Wonderful eating, Chinese style!—

In large skillet heat 2 tablespoons salad
oil; when piping hot, add 1 pound Chinese
podded peas* (in the pods) and 1 cup
sliced mushrooms. Cook and stir for 1 minute. Remove from heat.

Combine 2 tablespoons cornstarch, 2
teaspoons sugar, ¼ cup water, 3 tablespoons soy sauce, and 2 tablespoons cooking sherry; mix thoroughly with 5 cups
coarsely diced cooked chicken.

In another skillet or Dutch oven, heat ¼
cup salad oil; when hot, add the chicken
mixture. Cook, stirring constantly 2 minutes. Add three 5-ounce cans water chest-
nuts, drained and sliced very thin, and two
5-ounce cans bamboo shoots, drained and
sliced. Cook and stir 1 to 2 minutes.

Add Chinese peas, mushrooms, 2 tablespoons soy sauce, and 2 teaspoons salt.
Cook and stir about 3 minutes longer or
till hot through. Pass a cruet of soy sauce
and serve with Chinese Fried Rice. Makes
16 servings.

*You eat these pods and all. Instead of
shelling them, cook like green beans. Edi-
ble podded peas, also called podded sugar
peas in seed catalogs, are a favorite with
many home gardeners.

Or you can use two or three 7-ounce
packages of frozen Chinese pea pods. Pour
boiling water over frozen pea pods to
separate; drain. Cook as above.

Serve fresh pineapple sliced, diced, or in the shell—

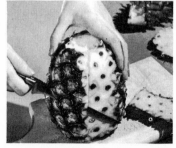

1 To *slice* or *dice*, first remove stem; hold onto pineapple with one hand and stem with the other;
twist firmly in opposite directions.   **2** With sharp knife, cut off base; stand upright. Pare strips
from top to bottom. Remove eyes with tip of paring knife, hard center with apple corer. Slice
fruit in rings, or dice.   **3** To *serve in shell*: Quarter fruit (and stem). Core. With grapefruit knife,
cut fruit from peel. Slice crosswise; zigzag slices as shown below.

Casserole supper for 24

Hamburger-Corn Casserole

4 pounds ground beef
3 medium onions, chopped (3 cups)
3 12-ounce cans whole kernel corn
3 cans condensed cream of chicken soup
3 cans condensed cream of mushroom
    soup
3 cups dairy sour cream
¾ cup chopped pimiento
2 teaspoons salt
1½ teaspoons monosodium glutamate
¾ teaspoon pepper
9 cups medium noodles, cooked,
    drained

Brown meat. Add onion; cook till tender but not brown. Add *drained* corn and next 7 ingredients. Mix well. Add noodles. Pour into two 13x9x2⅝-inch cake pans.

For *Crumb Topping*, combine 3 cups soft bread crumbs, ½ cup butter, melted, and ¾ teaspoon paprika. Sprinkle across casserole in diagonal rows. Bake at 350° about 45 minutes or till hot. Top with ¾ cup chopped parsley. Makes 24 servings.

Tangy Butter Sauce

Cream 1 cup butter or margarine; gradually add 2 cups sifted confectioners' sugar; cream thoroughly. Stir 2 cups cold water into 2 tablespoons cornstarch; cook and stir till thick and clear.

Stir hot mixture into creamed mixture. Add 2 teaspoons vinegar and 3 teaspoons vanilla. Serve warm. Makes 3⅓ cups.

Arctic Salad Slices

2 3-ounce packages cream cheese
2 tablespoons mayonnaise or salad
    dressing
2 tablespoons sugar

• • •

1 1-pound can (2 cups) whole-cranberry sauce
1 9-ounce can (1 cup) crushed
    pineapple or pineapple tidbits,
    drained
½ cup chopped California walnuts
1 cup whipping cream, whipped

Soften cheese; blend in mayonnaise and sugar. Add fruits and nuts. Fold in whipped cream. Pour into 8½x4½x2½-inch loaf pan. Freeze firm, 6 hours or overnight.

To serve, let stand at room temperature about 15 minutes; turn out on lettuce; slice. Makes 8 servings. (Make 3 salad loaves for 24 servings.)

Gingerbread

Bake two when you're serving 24—

½ cup shortening
½ cup sugar
1 egg
½ cup light molasses

• • •

1½ cups sifted all-purpose flour
¾ teaspoon salt
¾ teaspoon soda
½ teaspoon ginger
½ teaspoon cinnamon

• • •

½ cup boiling water

Stir shortening to soften. Gradually add sugar, creaming till light and fluffy. Add egg and molasses; beat thoroughly. Sift together dry ingredients; add to molasses mixture alternately with boiling water, beating after each addition.

Bake in well-greased 8x8x2-inch pan in moderate oven (350°) about 35 to 40 minutes or till done. Cut in 12 pieces. Serve warm with Tangy Butter Sauce.

Index